Charts

POMEGRANATE ARTBOOKS
SAN FRANCISCO

a book of postcards

Pomegranate Publications
Box 808022
Petaluma, CA 94975

© 1989 Michael Ochs Archives

ISBN 0-87654-425-1

Cover design by Marianne Birt
Printed in Korea

Sheb Wooley's "The Purple People Eater" hit number one on the pop charts in 1958, just one year after Pat Boone's "Love Letters in the Sand" enjoyed the same status. Frank Sinatra had a number-one hit, "Learnin' the Blues," in 1955, the same year that Bill Haley and the Comets burst on the scene with "Rock Around the Clock." Sam Cooke was heard on all of the pop stations singing "You Send Me" in 1957, while Danny and the Juniors' "At the Hop" hit the top of the charts that same year.

The 1950s encompassed a decade of change in popular music. Rock and roll found its beginnings on the same radio stations that aired the soothing melodies of the ballad singers and crooners. Everyone was listening to everything. It wasn't until the '60s that radio stations made choices to narrow their selection of music in response to the growth of rock and roll and a new generation.

But the decade of the '50s continues to be remembered as the melting pot of musical multiple personalities. The thirty postcards of photographs of 1950s successful pop chart musicians in this collection from the Michael Ochs Archives showcase the extreme diversity in the popular music of the time—music that today has proved to be more long-lasting than much that followed it.

The '50s: Top of the Charts
The Everly Brothers
"Wake Up Little Susie," 1957
"All I Have to Do Is Dream," 1958
"Bird Dog," 1958

POMEGRANATE • BOX 808022 • PETALUMA, CA 94975

Photograph courtesy Michael Ochs Archives

The '50s: Top of the Charts
Buddy Holly and the Crickets
"That'll Be the Day," 1957

POMEGRANATE • BOX 808022 • PETALUMA, CA 94975

Photograph courtesy Michael Ochs Archives

The '50s: Top of the Charts
Pat Boone (b. 1934)
"Ain't That a Shame," 1955
"I Almost Lost My Mind," 1956
"Don't Forbid Me," 1956
"Love Letters in the Sand," 1957
"April Love," 1957

POMEGRANATE • BOX 808022 • PETALUMA, CA 94975

Photograph courtesy Michael Ochs Archives

The '50s: Top of the Charts
Tommy Edwards (1922–69)
"It's All in the Game," 1958

POMEGRANATE • BOX 808022 • PETALUMA, CA 94975

Photograph courtesy Michael Ochs Archives

The '50s: Top of the Charts
The Silhouettes
"Get a Job," 1958

POMEGRANATE • BOX 808022 • PETALUMA, CA 94975

Photograph courtesy Michael Ochs Archives

The '50s: Top of the Charts
Frank Sinatra (b. 1915)
"Learnin' the Blues," 1958

POMEGRANATE • BOX 808022 • PETALUMA, CA 94975

Photograph courtesy Michael Ochs Archives

The '50s: Top of the Charts
Johnny Mathis (b. 1935)
"Chances Are," 1957

POMEGRANATE • BOX 808022 • PETALUMA, CA 94975

Photograph courtesy Michael Ochs Archives

The '50s: Top of the Charts
Danny and the Juniors
"At the Hop," 1957

POMEGRANATE • BOX 808022 • PETALUMA, CA 94975

Photograph courtesy Michael Ochs Archives

The '50s: Top of the Charts
Lloyd Price (b. 1933)
"Stagger Lee," 1958

POMEGRANATE • BOX 808022 • PETALUMA, CA 94975

Photograph courtesy Michael Ochs Archives

The '50s: Top of the Charts
Frankie Avalon (b. 1939)
"Venus," 1959
"Why," 1959

POMEGRANATE • BOX 808022 • PETALUMA, CA 94975

Photograph courtesy Michael Ochs Archives

The '50s: Top of the Charts
The Coasters
"Yakety-Yak," 1958

POMEGRANATE • BOX 808022 • PETALUMA, CA 94975

Photograph courtesy Michael Ochs Archives

The '50s: Top of the Charts
Jimmie Rodgers (b. 1933)
"Honeycomb," 1957

POMEGRANATE • BOX 808022 • PETALUMA, CA 94975

Photograph courtesy Michael Ochs Archives

The '50s: Top of the Charts
Sonny James (b. 1929)
"Young Love," 1956

POMEGRANATE • BOX 808022 • PETALUMA, CA 94975

Photograph courtesy Michael Ochs Archives

The '50s: Top of the Charts
The Fleetwoods
"Come Softly to Me," 1959
"Mr. Blue," 1959

POMEGRANATE • BOX 808022 • PETALUMA, CA 94975

Photograph courtesy Michael Ochs Archives

The '50s: Top of the Charts
Sam Cooke (1935–64)
"You Send Me," 1957

POMEGRANATE • BOX 808022 • PETALUMA, CA 94975

Photograph courtesy Michael Ochs Archives

The '50s: Top of the Charts
Mark Dinning (1933–86)
"Teen Angel," 1959

POMEGRANATE • BOX 808022 • PETALUMA, CA 94975

Photograph courtesy Michael Ochs Archives

The '50s: Top of the Charts
Conway Twitty (b. 1933)
"It's Only Make Believe," 1958

POMEGRANATE • BOX 808022 • PETALUMA, CA 94975

Photograph courtesy Michael Ochs Archives

The '50s: Top of the Charts
The McGuire Sisters
"Sincerely," 1955
"Sugartime," 1957

POMEGRANATE • BOX 808022 • PETALUMA, CA 94975

Photograph courtesy Michael Ochs Archives

The '50s: Top of the Charts
Paul Anka (b. 1941)
"Diana," 1957
"Lonely Boy," 1959

POMEGRANATE • BOX 808022 • PETALUMA, CA 94975

Photograph courtesy Michael Ochs Archives

The '50s: Top of the Charts
Marty Robbins (1925–82)
"El Paso," 1959

POMEGRANATE • BOX 808022 • PETALUMA, CA 94975

Photograph courtesy Michael Ochs Archives

The '50s: Top of the Charts
The Platters
"The Great Pretender," 1955
"My Prayer," 1956
"Twilight Time," 1958
"Smoke Gets in Your Eyes," 1958

POMEGRANATE • BOX 808022 • PETALUMA, CA 94975

Photograph courtesy Michael Ochs Archives

The '50s: Top of the Charts
Georgia Gibbs (b. 1920)
"Dance With Me, Henry," 1955

POMEGRANATE • BOX 808022 • PETALUMA, CA 94975

Photograph courtesy Michael Ochs Archives

The '50s: Top of the Charts
Ricky Nelson (1940–85)
"Poor Little Fool," 1958

POMEGRANATE • BOX 808022 • PETALUMA, CA 94975

Photograph courtesy Michael Ochs Archives

The '50s: Top of the Charts
The Champs
"Tequila," 1958

POMEGRANATE • BOX 808022 • PETALUMA, CA 94975

Photograph courtesy Michael Ochs Archives

The '50s: Top of the Charts
Wilbert Harrison (b. 1929)
"Kansas City," 1959

POMEGRANATE • BOX 808022 • PETALUMA, CA 94975

Photograph courtesy Michael Ochs Archives

The '50s: Top of the Charts
Sheb Wooley (b. 1921)
"The Purple People Eater," 1958

POMEGRANATE • BOX 808022 • PETALUMA, CA 94975

Photograph courtesy Michael Ochs Archives

The '50s: Top of the Charts
Bobby Darin (1936–73)
"Mack the Knife," 1959

POMEGRANATE • BOX 808022 • PETALUMA, CA 94975

Photograph courtesy Michael Ochs Archives

The '50s: Top of the Charts
Santo and Johnny
"Sleep Walk," 1959

POMEGRANATE • BOX 808022 • PETALUMA, CA 94975

Photograph courtesy Michael Ochs Archives

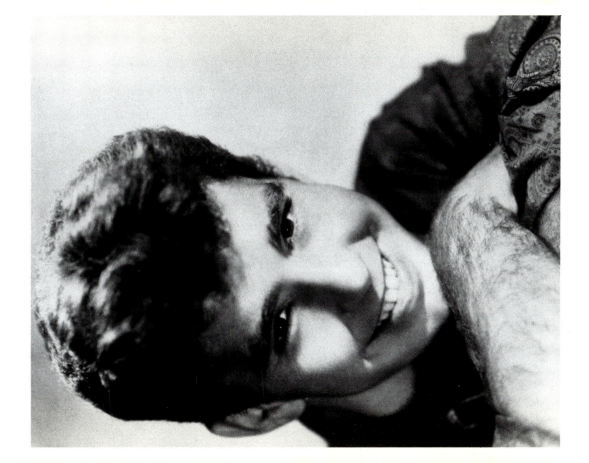

The '50s: Top of the Charts
Buddy Knox (b. 1933)
"Party Doll," 1957

POMEGRANATE • BOX 808022 • PETALUMA, CA 94975

Photograph courtesy Michael Ochs Archives

The '50s: Top of the Charts
Bill Haley and the Comets
"Rock Around the Clock," 1955

POMEGRANATE • BOX 808022 • PETALUMA, CA 94975

Photograph courtesy Michael Ochs Archives